Now I know that my mother fled because of severe depression. But I did not know that when I was seven, and so in those months that followed her abandoning us, deep wounds opened up in my heart. The only person I had ever loved or trusted had abandoned me. Her betrayal hit me like a tsunami, and cut deep grooves of fear, panic, grief, and despair in me. And something bitter and dark took root: hatred. I grew to hate the one person I had ever loved. She had destroyed me, and now I wanted to kill her.

Meanwhile, my aunt took her anger at my mother out on me, as I was the oldest. She constantly beat me, locking me in her chicken coop at night with only a burlap sack for cover, as I was forbidden to go into her house.

When I was twelve years old, I began to run away. I had discovered that the white people had rubbish bins behind their houses which often had stale or rotting food in them. I began to live out of these rubbish bins, for the food there was better than what my aunt gave me. I dug a hole in the sand beneath a bridge and slept there at night, with my burlap sack for cover. It was cleaner than the chicken coop.

Black Shadows

Lonely, depressed, and fearful, I even attempted to hang myself from a tree one day. Someone saw me and called for help and I ended up in hospital. I was heartbroken when the nurses finally made me leave that nice clean bed – the first I had ever slept in.

No wonder, that when some nice young men met me as I roamed about the township and showed me some kindness, I went along to their Marxist training camp in the bush. Here they had gathered other homeless young men like me. As all of us were simple and uneducated, the Marxists could not teach us anything complicated. So, they simply told us that it was the government, the whites and the Christians who had made our lives so miserable, and that we should fight back. They encouraged us to cause trouble whenever we could – to throw petrol bombs, and to cause civil unrest.

This sounded great to me. The simple truth – that my family's troubles had nothing to do with the government, the whites or the Christians – did not occur to me. All I thought was that now, at last, I could do something to express my anger and hatred. We formed a gang called the Black Shadows and I was the leader. We carried out numerous vicious attacks on various people and places in Highfield. It made us feel cool, and successful to know that we were feared and hated.

One night I was leading my Black Shadows towards the Machipisa Shopping Centre. We were going to throw petrol bombs at a bank, to stir up some trouble. Why not? We hated everyone, especially the police and the rich.

But on the way to the shopping centre, we passed a field that had a large billowy white tent on it, and there were lots of people milling about. There was music coming from inside. Was it a circus?

Then we heard hymns being sung, and someone read aloud the sign: Dorothea Mission. Christians! One of us suggested we could throw our petrol bombs into the tent full of people. And so I told my gang to wait for a few minutes, while I went inside to investigate.

Inside, an usher tried to give me a seat, but I snarled at him, and he backed away. A young woman stood up to speak. She was so pretty that I just stood and stared. She told about how Jesus had met her in the slums of Soweto, and turned her life around. Then a man stood up and stared at us. He seemed distressed, and startled me by suddenly declaring that many of us would die and be lost for ever!

Had he guessed why I was there? He went on to say that all of us were without hope in the world, and on our own. That all of us had done wrong things, and we knew that we had. We had no way to get rid of the evil things we had done – we were all totally guilty. As he spoke, all the past bad things that I had done came back to me, and I could feel my desperation and my anger rising. I wanted to kill him. I would kill him!

Explosion

But suddenly the preacher switched again and began talking to us about Jesus. About how Jesus knew us, just as we were, and how He loved us anyway. So much so, that He had come to pay the price of our sin. If we turned to Him, he would forgive us that sin, and give us a whole new life. He cared for us, He accepted us. I could exchange my poverty and sin for Jesus' purity and riches. Tears for all the pain, loneliness, hatred and fear I had ever known began to flow down my cheeks. I could not bear this burden of my life any longer.
If Jesus could not help me now, I wanted to die.

Clutching my bag of petrol bombs, I stumbled forward, wanting to reach the preacher. I was a very simple young man, and had no idea that this might startle him, or that it was not allowed. I just wanted Jesus – now. People tried to stop me, but the preacher saw the desperation in my face, and told them to let me come. I knelt in front of him with my petrol bombs and cried and cried as he carried on preaching.

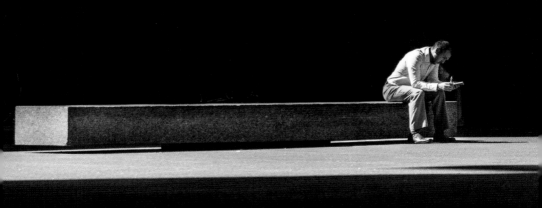

Then suddenly there was an explosion. Tired of waiting for me, my gang members had thrown stones and then a petrol bomb at the outside of the tent. In the confusion that followed, as the fire was put out and as people fled the meeting, the preacher could no longer preach, and so he began to talk to me. He wanted to know my story, and I blurted out the misery of my life: my father's rejection and brutality, my mother's abandonment of me, and my aunt's cruelty. The panic and pain of the rejection poured out of me. I knew everyone in the world hated me, and I hated them.

Take Me Up!

To my astonishment, the preacher's eyes filled with tears. "Young man," he said, "my mother was about 14 when she got pregnant. The young man who had done this to her did not want to know. When the child was born, my mother did not want me either. When I was two weeks old, she wrapped me in a blanket and stuffed me down a toilet and left me to die. Another woman came in and found me in time, and took me to hospital. I have no idea who my mother was, or who my father was. Like you, neither of them ever wanted me."

I stared at the preacher in astonishment. He had all the signs of being loved, secure and at peace with himself. This was not possible. But the preacher was thumbing through his Bible. "Listen," he said. "This is what God and his son Jesus Christ has to say to people like me and like you. It is a promise that He has made to us. It is in Psalm 27:10: 'Though my father and my mother forsake me, the Lord will take me up.'"

The words rang in my head: God and Jesus had made me this promise: "the Lord would take me up."

Teach Me Your Way

Hear, O Lord, when I cry aloud,
    be gracious to me and answer me!
'Come,' my heart says, 'seek his face!'
    Your face, LORD, do I seek.
     Do not hide your face from me.
Do not turn your servant away in anger,
    you who have been my help.
Do not cast me off, do not forsake me,
    O God of my salvation!
If my father and mother forsake me,
    the LORD will take me up.
Teach me your way, O LORD,
    and lead me on a level path
    because of my enemies.
Do not give me up to the will of my adversaries,
    for false witnesses have risen against me,
    and they are breathing out violence.
I believe that I shall see the goodness of the LORD
    in the land of the living.
Wait for the LORD;
    be strong, and let your heart take courage;
    wait for the LORD!

Psalm 27:7-14 (NRSV)

The Book of Psalms is part of the Bible. The Psalms give us words to praise God and to pray.

Ready to Live

Hearing this verse was the changing point of my life. No one was denying my pain, but instead God was offering his own love. I knelt to approach God for the first time in my life. "God," I cried. "I have nothing. I am nothing. I can't read. I can't write. My parents don't want me. Take me up, God, take me up. I'm sorry for the bad things I've done. Jesus, forgive me, and take me now."

Immediately I felt as if a heavy burden had rolled off my back. There was a tremendous rush of relief and peace. I was astonished at the joy that flowed through me. Me – a thrown-away child among the millions of Africa, but Jesus had found me.

Slowly I became aware of people nearby, needing the preacher to help them calm the chaos. I told him that I would go now, that I had found Jesus.

He said to me, "Yes, you are ready to die now. But for the first time, you are also ready to live! God bless you!"

New Life

Outside the tent, I dodged the crowds and the police and the members of my gang. I lay flat on the grass so that no one would see me, and then I crawled away.

For a while I wandered aimlessly on the outskirts of New Highfield township, dazed and wanting to be alone. I could not go back to the gang's hideout, so instead I made my way back to my old place under the bridge. I crept into my hole and covered myself with the bit of sacking, and then scooped the sand back on top of me.

Far above me was the arch of the bridge, and far beyond that, the shining stars. For the first time in my life, I did not feel alone. The loving presence of Jesus was around me like a soft blanket. I prayed, 'God, I've never been to school. I can't read. I can't even write my name. But I want to spend the rest of my life telling people about you.' I did not then know that the word 'evangelist' existed, but that was what I wanted to do for the rest of my life. At last at peace, I drifted off to sleep.

The next morning when the bird song woke me, I discovered that the loving presence of God was still with me. I wandered about quietly, rejoicing and praying to him. I even leaned against a tree and hugged it, I was so happy!

Suddenly a voice in my head said, 'Stephen, stand up!' Astonished, I backed away from the tree. Was I going crazy? 'Stephen,' the voice in my head continued: 'I will send you to the nations that you do not know.'

That was all. I stood in the bright sunshine in awe. I did not doubt that Jesus had just spoken to me, and that he had given me my life's work to do. The first thing I needed was to put my old life in order.

New Habits

In the weeks that followed my conversion, my life turned upside-down. I went to the police to confess my crimes and to tell them that I had met Jesus. The police did not know what to do with me, so they gave me money to buy a Bible. I bought a Bible in Shona and carried it everywhere, though I could not read. Finally, a white missionary, Johannes Joubert, found me and took me into his care. He made up a bed for me in his garage, and taught me to have a bath, use a knife and fork, to speak and to read English and Shona. He saw my passion to be an evangelist, and he was determined to help me.

We had many ups and downs. New habits are hard to form, and I often struggled with my old bitterness and anger. But, like the tide going out, gradually my heart was drained of its anger and swirling undertow of bitterness and violence. In their place, an attitude of peace, love and forgiveness began to flow in. The light of Christ glowed brighter and brighter in my heart.

And so it was that I did become an evangelist. I preached all over Africa, throughout America and Europe, and was privileged to lead many thousands of people to faith in Jesus Christ.

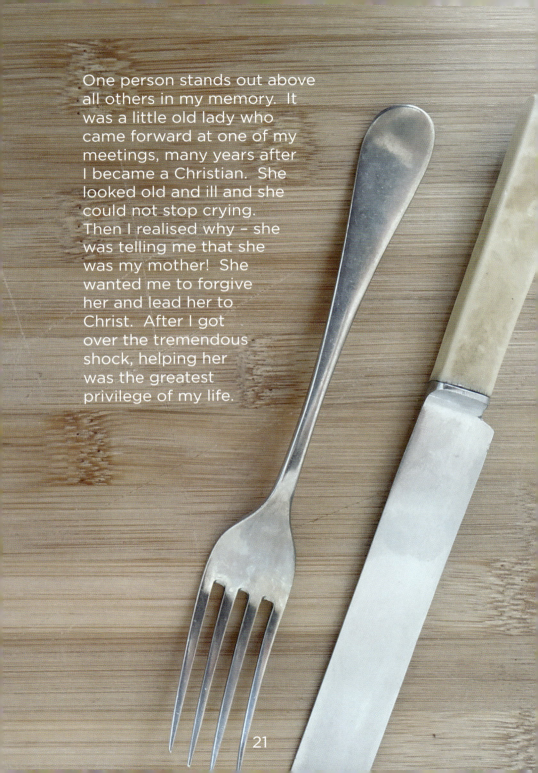

One person stands out above all others in my memory. It was a little old lady who came forward at one of my meetings, many years after I became a Christian. She looked old and ill and she could not stop crying. Then I realised why – she was telling me that she was my mother! She wanted me to forgive her and lead her to Christ. After I got over the tremendous shock, helping her was the greatest privilege of my life.

Pray Now

Years earlier, I had married a lovely Christian woman and had several children. We were a stable, happy family, and so we invited my mother to come and live with us, which she did. I thought that my life was complete until God reminded me that I had had a father, too. I found him in a remote village, very, very old. In time, he became a Christian too.

A highlight of my life as an evangelist has been to begin the annual Presidential Prayer Breakfast in Malawi. When I stand up and speak before the president, I look back on the little, scared, ignorant boy that used to live in a chicken coop, and thank God for his love that has delivered me, and brought me into this wide and spacious existence.

Wherever you are, and whatever terrible things may have happened in your life, you don't need to live with them forever. The past does not own you – it may be where you came from, but it does not have to be where you spend your present, or your future.

Jesus can forgive your sins and transform your life so that you can forgive others, and become the person He intended you to be. He loves you and accepts you just as you are. He is ready to hear your prayer.